T3-BHM-785

Michael Faraday

by MARY BETH SPANN
With the Editors of TIME FOR KIDS

Table of Contents

CHAPTER 1
A SCIENTIST'S BEGINNINGS

An Unlikely Scientist

Michael Faraday did not seem like he would become a great **scientist**. His family was poor. He had little schooling, or education. But his discoveries about electricity changed the world!

Michael Faraday as a young man

Faraday was born near London, England, on September 22, 1791. His father was a blacksmith. His father was often sick. He could not work. Faraday's family did not have a lot of food. Sometimes they had just one loaf of bread for an entire week.

Faraday learned how to read, write, and work with numbers when he was a boy. He loved to read. Faraday read about science. He said that reading allowed him to teach himself science. This helped him become a great scientist.

---

blacksmith: a person who works with metal

London in the early 1800s

Birth of a Bookworm

Faraday left school when he was about fourteen. He needed to make money for his family. Faraday became George Reibau's apprentice, or helper. Reibau put books together. He was a bookbinder.

Reibau taught Faraday how to put books together. In his free time, Faraday read many of the books that he worked on. He liked the encyclopedia and science books best. A family friend said that Faraday was "the best bookworm for eating his way to the inside [of books]!"

Reibau wanted Faraday to study science. He let Faraday do experiments with **static electricity**.

bookworm: a person who reads many books

A bookbinder from the 1800s

Reibau told Faraday to take notes of what he read. Faraday took notes for the rest of his life. Scientists still read his notes today.

Jane Marcet wrote a book called *Conversations in Chemistry*. This book influenced Faraday. Marcet wrote the book for young people. It was easy to understand. The book taught Faraday about **chemistry**.

The book taught Faraday how to explain scientific ideas <u>simply</u> and clearly. People understood Faraday's ideas because he explained them so well.

Clue: The word *simply* is an adverb. Adverbs modify adjectives, verbs, and adverbs. On this page, *simply* modifies the verb *explain*. Can you find another adverb on this page?

> ### Faraday in Focus
> Faraday described how his reading had changed him. "I could believe in…[fairy tales] as easily as in the encyclopedia. But facts were important and saved me. I could trust a fact."

Shocking!

Have you ever petted a cat's fur? Did you hear crackling sounds? Have you walked on a carpet and then felt a shock when you touched a doorknob? This happens because of small energy particles, called **electrons**. The electrons "jump" from one surface to another. This is a form of electricity called static electricity.

Faraday Speaks Out

Faraday wanted to teach science. He wanted to speak to people. He wanted to speak well. He asked a friend to help him improve his grammar. He studied grammar two hours a week for seven years! Faraday asked for help with learning. This helped him become a better scientist.

In 1810, Faraday joined a club to talk about many kinds of ideas. He was nineteen years old. The club members helped him think about many scientific ideas. Faraday gave his first science speeches, or talks, at club meetings.

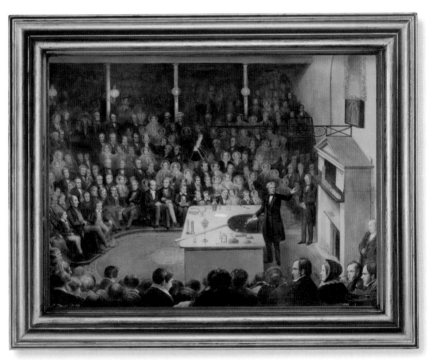

Faraday speaks about science.

Meeting an Important Chemist

In 1812, Faraday went to some talks about chemistry. Sir Humphrey Davy spoke. Davy was an important chemist. Faraday liked his talks. Faraday took many notes. Faraday wanted to work with Davy. Faraday made a book of his notes about Davy's talks. He sent the book and a letter to Davy. In the letter, Faraday asked Davy for work. At first, there were no jobs for Faraday. Then, one day Davy gave Faraday a job as his assistant, or helper.

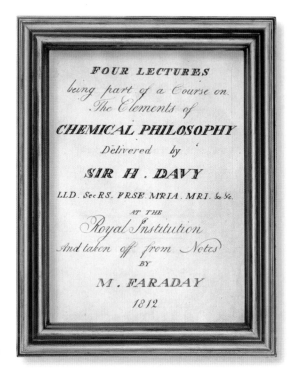

Ideas at Work!

A **theory** is an idea that helps explain things. Scientists have theories about the way things work, change, move, live, or grow. Scientists do experiments to test their theories. They explain their theories to other scientists. This helps them show if a theory works.

CHAPTER 2

NEW DISCOVERIES AHEAD

Time for Travel

Faraday worked with Davy. They traveled to France and other countries in Europe. There was a war in Europe at the time. Davy and Faraday had to ask Napoleon Bonaparte to travel to Europe. Bonaparte was the famous ruler of France.

Faraday and Davy used this instrument in their light experiments.

Faraday did some chemistry research for Davy in Europe. Faraday and Davy did an experiment in Italy. They set a diamond on fire. They heated the diamond with rays from the Sun. In the experiment, they made sunlight pass through two giant lenses.

Faraday knew a lot about chemistry when he finished working with Davy.

Faraday in Focus
Faraday took notes about his trips with Davy. He wrote 400 pages about their trips and discoveries.

What Is Chemistry?

Do you spend time inside buildings? Do you ride in cars? Do you buy clothes? Do you eat food from the supermarket? If you answered "yes" to any of those questions, you can thank chemistry.

Chemistry gives people the materials that make buildings, cars, clothes, and food. Chemistry is the study of elements and how they join together.

Elements are metals and nonmetals. Elements cannot be broken down. Metals are solids. They have a definite shape. They take up a definite amount of space. They can conduct, or carry, electricity. Iron, copper, and zinc are three important elements that are metals. Nonmetals (except carbon) do not carry electricity. Hydrogen and oxygen are nonmetal elements.

Today, scientists know about more than 110 elements. Scientists are discovering more elements all the time. Most elements can be mixed with other elements. Together they make **compounds**. Some compounds are natural. Water is a natural compound. It is made of hydrogen and oxygen. Scientists make compounds, too.

Faraday used a chemical set like this in his experiments.

9

On to Electricity

In 1820, Faraday wanted to know more about the work of Hans Christian Oersted. Oersted discovered the link between **electricity** and **magnetism**. He found out that electricity moving through a wire could move a magnetic needle in a <u>compass</u>.

This is a diagram of one of Faraday's electromagnetism experiments.

Electromagnets are magnets that use electricity. You can make an electromagnet by putting wire around a magnetic material like iron. When an electrical current flows through the wire, the material becomes a magnet.

Faraday did more than Oersted. In 1821, Faraday invented the first electric motor! Faraday was interested in electricity and magnetism. But he spent the next ten years talking to people about science.

People use Faraday's discoveries to make modern electric motors.

compass: a tool used to find direction

Days of Discovery

In 1831, Faraday decided to study electricity and magnetism again. Faraday made an interesting discovery in ten days. He discovered that a magnetic field could control an **electrical current**. This meant that electricity could run machines. The current could be moved back and forth or turned on and off. Today, **technology** based on Faraday's discoveries are used in machines like trains and microphones.

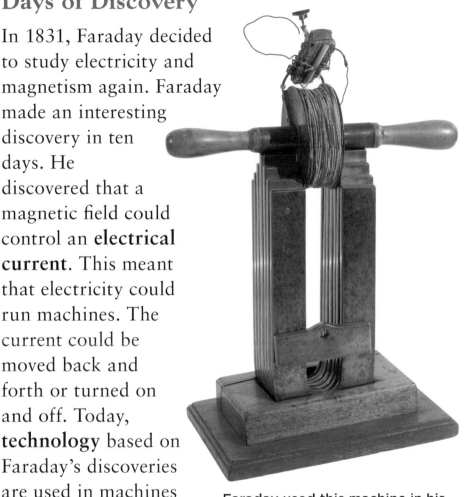

Faraday used this machine in his experiment with electricity and magnetism in 1831.

Faraday in Focus
Faraday helped invent the words *electrode*, *electrolyte*, *anode*, *cathode*, and *ion*. Use a dictionary to find out what these words mean.

CHAPTER 3
A GIFT TO SCIENCE

A Brighter Light

In 1836, Faraday was named Scientific Advisor to Trinity House. Trinity House <u>was</u>, and still is, in charge of safe boating around the shores of England and Wales. At that time, lighthouses

Lighthouse

used lamps that burned oil. Faraday thought that the lighthouses could be better.

In the early 1840s, Faraday invented a better chimney that burned oil. People put this invention in lighthouses and important buildings. Buckingham Palace had one. The British Royal family lives there.

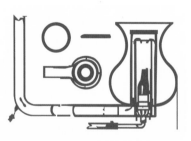

A drawing of Faraday's design for an oil-burning chimney

<u>Clue</u>: <u>Was</u> is the irregular past tense of the verb *to be*. Can you find one more irregular past tense verb on this page?

Final Years

In the early 1840s, Faraday became <u>ill</u>. But he continued to do science experiments. He discovered that a magnetic force could change light. He put a piece of glass at the end of a strong electromagnet. Then he passed light through the glass. The light changed when he turned on the electromagnet. Faraday tried the experiment again. This time he hung the glass. The glass moved. This told Faraday that the magnetic force affected the light and the glass. He found that all matter has a magnetic force. This discovery was called the Faraday Effect.

<u>ill</u>: not healthy, sick

Faraday's discoveries helped make many forms of modern communication possible.

Michael Faraday's Journal

Michael Faraday died on August 25, 1867. He left about 4,800 notes and letters. His notes tell the story of his life. His letters went to scientists and political leaders around the world.

A page from Michael Faraday's journal

Faraday's writings let us look into his mind. We know what he did in his experiments. We do not have to guess. People read his writings today to learn about his love for science and his discoveries.

Write What You Learn!

Here is how to keep a notebook or journal like Michael Faraday's!
- Write every day. Write the date first.
- Use simple language. Write in ink.
- Number the pages.
- Write what you learn each day. Write how you learned it.
- Use a new page every day.
- Make drawings if you want.
- Read all of your notes again. You will see how much you have learned!

Glossary

chemistry the science that studies the nature of substances *(page 5)*

compound two or more elements joined together *(page 9)*

electrical current the flow of an electrical charge *(page 11)*

electricity energy made by the flow of electrons *(page 10)*

electron a particle outside the nucleus (center) of an atom *(page 5)*

magnetism a force that attracts iron, steel, or other metals *(page 10)*

scientist a person who studies living things or the world by measuring, testing, and experimenting *(page 2)*

static electricity the buildup of an electrical charge on a material *(page 4)*

technology use of science for practical purposes *(page 11)*

theory ideas that explain something but need to be tested to see if they are true *(page 7)*

Index